Tarot &
Daily One
Card Draw

This Journal Belongs To

_____

_____

_____

Strategic Publications

Evening Reflection

Date: _____   Deck: _____

Question: _____
_____

Card: _____
  ○ Upright   ○ Reversed

Keywords: _____
_____

Standard Meaning: _____
_____

Initial Thoughts

Intuitive Interpretation

Emotional Response

How did this card play out today?

Evening Reflection

Date: _____ Deck: _____

Question: _____

_____

Card: _____

◯ Upright   ◯ Reversed

Keywords: _____

_____

Standard Meaning: _____

_____

Initial Thoughts

Intuitive Interpretation

Emotional Response

How did this card play out today?

Date: _____   Deck: _____

Question: _____

_____

Card: _____

◯ Upright   ◯ Reversed

Keywords: _____

_____

Standard Meaning: _____

_____

Initial Thoughts

Intuitive Interpretation

Emotional Response

How did this card play out today?

Date: _____ Deck: _____

Question: _____

_____

Card: _____

○ Upright ○ Reversed

Keywords: _____

_____

Standard Meaning: _____

_____

Initial Thoughts

Intuitive Interpretation

Emotional Response

How did this card play out today?

Date: _____   Deck: _____

Question: _____
_____

Card: _____

○ Upright   ○ Reversed

Keywords: _____
_____

Standard Meaning: _____
_____

Initial Thoughts

Intuitive Interpretation

Emotional Response

How did this card play out today?

Evening Reflection

Date: _____   Deck: _____

Question: _____

_____

Card: _____

○ Upright   ○ Reversed

Keywords: _____

_____

Standard Meaning: _____

_____

Initial Thoughts

Intuitive Interpretation

Emotional Response

How did this card play out today?

Evening Reflection

Date: _____ Deck: _____

Question: _____
_____

Card: _____
  ○ Upright   ○ Reversed

Keywords: _____
_____

Standard Meaning: _____
_____

Initial Thoughts

Intuitive Interpretation

Emotional Response

How did this card play out today?

Evening Reflection

Date: _____   Deck: _____

Question: _____

_____

Card: _____

○ Upright   ○ Reversed

Keywords: _____
_____

Standard Meaning: _____
_____

Initial Thoughts

Intuitive Interpretation

Emotional Response

How did this card play out today?

Evening Reflection

Date: _____   Deck: _____

Question: _____
_____

Card: _____

◯ Upright   ◯ Reversed

Keywords: _____
_____

Standard Meaning: _____
_____

Initial Thoughts

Intuitive Interpretation

Emotional Response

How did this card play out today?

Evening Reflection

Date: _____   Deck: _____

Question: _____

_____

Card: _____

◯ Upright   ◯ Reversed

Keywords: _____

_____

Standard Meaning: _____

_____

Initial Thoughts

Intuitive Interpretation

Emotional Response

How did this card play out today?

Date: _____ Deck: _____

Question: _____

_____

Card: _____

○ Upright   ○ Reversed

Keywords: _____

_____

Standard Meaning: _____

_____

Initial Thoughts

Intuitive Interpretation

Emotional Response

How did this card play out today?

Date: _____   Deck: _____

Question: _____

_____

Card: _____

◯ Upright   ◯ Reversed

Keywords: _____

_____

Standard Meaning: _____

_____

Initial Thoughts

Intuitive Interpretation

Emotional Response

How did this card play out today?

Date: _____   Deck: _____

Question: _____
_____

Card: _____
  ○ Upright   ○ Reversed

Keywords: _____
_____

Standard Meaning: _____
_____

Initial Thoughts

Intuitive Interpretation

Emotional Response

How did this card play out today?

Evening Reflection

Date: _____   Deck: _____

Question: _____

_____

Card: _____

    ○ Upright   ○ Reversed

Keywords: _____

_____

Standard Meaning: _____

_____

Initial Thoughts

Intuitive Interpretation

Emotional Response

How did this card play out today?

Date: _____   Deck: _____

Question: _____

_____

Card: _____

○ Upright   ○ Reversed

Keywords: _____

_____

Standard Meaning: _____

_____

Initial Thoughts

Intuitive Interpretation

Emotional Response

How did this card play out today?

Evening Reflection

Date: _____   Deck: _____

Question: _____

_____

Card: _____

⊙ Upright   ⊙ Reversed

Keywords: _____

_____

Standard Meaning: _____

_____

Initial Thoughts

Intuitive Interpretation

Emotional Response

How did this card play out today?

Date: _____ Deck: _____

Question: _____

_____

Card: _____

○ Upright   ○ Reversed

Keywords: _____

_____

Standard Meaning: _____

_____

Initial Thoughts

Intuitive Interpretation

Emotional Response

How did this card play out today?

Date: _____   Deck: _____

Question: _____

_____

Card: _____

○ Upright   ○ Reversed

Keywords: _____

_____

Standard Meaning: _____

_____

Initial Thoughts

Intuitive Interpretation

Emotional Response

How did this card play out today?

Date: _____   Deck: _____

Question: _____

_____

Card: _____
⊙ Upright   ⊙ Reversed

Keywords: _____
_____

Standard Meaning: _____
_____

| Initial Thoughts |

| Intuitive Interpretation |

| Emotional Response |

| How did this card play out today? |

Evening Reflection

Date: _____   Deck: _____

Question: _____
_____

Card: _____
  ○ Upright   ○ Reversed

Keywords: _____
_____

Standard Meaning: _____
_____

Initial Thoughts

Intuitive Interpretation

Emotional Response

How did this card play out today?

Evening Reflection

Date: _____   Deck: _____

Question: _____

_____

Card: _____

⭘ Upright   ⭘ Reversed

Keywords: _____
_____

Standard Meaning: _____
_____

Initial Thoughts

Intuitive Interpretation

Emotional Response

How did this card play out today?

Evening Reflection

Date: _____   Deck: _____

Question: _____

_____

Card: _____

    ○ Upright   ○ Reversed

Keywords: _____

_____

Standard Meaning: _____

_____

Initial Thoughts

Intuitive Interpretation

Emotional Response

How did this card play out today?

Date: _____ Deck: _____

Question: _____

_____

Card: _____

    ◯ Upright   ◯ Reversed

Keywords: _____

_____

Standard Meaning: _____

_____

Initial Thoughts

Intuitive Interpretation

Emotional Response

How did this card play out today?

Evening Reflection

Date: _____ Deck: _____

Question: _____

_____

Card: _____

○ Upright   ○ Reversed

Keywords: _____

_____

Standard Meaning: _____

_____

Initial Thoughts

Intuitive Interpretation

Emotional Response

How did this card play out today?

Date: _____   Deck: _____

Question: _____
_____

Card: _____
○ Upright   ○ Reversed

Keywords: _____
_____

Standard Meaning: _____
_____

Initial Thoughts

Intuitive Interpretation

Emotional Response

How did this card play out today?

Evening Reflection

Date: _____ Deck: _____

Question: _____

_____

Card: _____

◯ Upright   ◯ Reversed

Keywords: _____

_____

Standard Meaning: _____

_____

Initial Thoughts

Intuitive Interpretation

Emotional Response

How did this card play out today?

Date: _____   Deck: _____

Question: _____

_____

Card: _____

⚪ Upright   ⚪ Reversed

Keywords: _____

_____

Standard Meaning: _____

_____

Initial Thoughts

Intuitive Interpretation

Emotional Response

How did this card play out today?

Evening Reflection

Date: _____ Deck: _____

Question: _____
_____

Card: _____
⚪ Upright   ⚪ Reversed

Keywords: _____
_____

Standard Meaning: _____
_____

| Initial Thoughts |

| Intuitive Interpretation |

| Emotional Response |

| How did this card play out today? |

Evening Reflection

Date: _____ Deck: _____

Question: _____

_____

Card: _____

◯ Upright   ◯ Reversed

Keywords: _____

_____

Standard Meaning: _____

_____

Initial Thoughts

Intuitive Interpretation

Emotional Response

How did this card play out today?

Evening Reflection

Date: _____   Deck: _____

Question: _____

_____

Card: _____
○ Upright   ○ Reversed

Keywords: _____
_____

Standard Meaning: _____
_____

Initial Thoughts

Intuitive Interpretation

Emotional Response

How did this card play out today?

Evening Reflection

Date: _____   Deck: _____

Question: _____

_____

Card: _____

      ○ Upright   ○ Reversed

Keywords: _____

_____

Standard Meaning: _____

_____

Initial Thoughts

Intuitive Interpretation

Emotional Response

How did this card play out today?

Evening Reflection

Date: _____   Deck: _____

Question: _____
_____

Card: _____
     ○ Upright   ○ Reversed

Keywords: _____
_____

Standard Meaning: _____
_____

Initial Thoughts

Intuitive Interpretation

Emotional Response

How did this card play out today?

Evening Reflection

Date: _____   Deck: _____

Question: _____

_____

Card: _____

○ Upright   ○ Reversed

Keywords: _____

_____

Standard Meaning: _____

_____

| Initial Thoughts |

| Intuitive Interpretation |

| Emotional Response |

| How did this card play out today? |

Evening Reflection

Date: _____   Deck: _____

Question: _____

_____

Card: _____

○ Upright   ○ Reversed

Keywords: _____
_____

Standard Meaning: _____
_____

Initial Thoughts

Intuitive Interpretation

Emotional Response

How did this card play out today?

Evening Reflection

Date: _____   Deck: _____

Question: _____

_____

Card: _____

○ Upright   ○ Reversed

Keywords: _____

_____

Standard Meaning: _____

_____

Initial Thoughts

Intuitive Interpretation

Emotional Response

How did this card play out today?

Evening Reflection

Date: _____   Deck: _____

Question: _____

_____

Card: _____

    ○ Upright   ○ Reversed

Keywords: _____

_____

Standard Meaning: _____

_____

Initial Thoughts

Intuitive Interpretation

Emotional Response

How did this card play out today?

Date: _____   Deck: _____

Question: _____

_____

Card: _____

     ◯ Upright   ◯ Reversed

Keywords: _____

_____

Standard Meaning: _____

_____

Initial Thoughts

Intuitive Interpretation

Emotional Response

How did this card play out today?

Evening Reflection

Date: _____ Deck: _____

Question: _____

_____

Card: _____

○ Upright   ○ Reversed

Keywords: _____

_____

Standard Meaning: _____

_____

| Initial Thoughts |

| Intuitive Interpretation |

| Emotional Response |

| How did this card play out today? |

Evening Reflection

Date: _____ Deck: _____

Question: _____
_____

Card: _____

○ Upright ○ Reversed

Keywords: _____
_____

Standard Meaning: _____
_____

Initial Thoughts

Intuitive Interpretation

Emotional Response

How did this card play out today?

Date: _____   Deck: _____

Question: _____
_____

Card: _____
○ Upright   ○ Reversed

Keywords: _____
_____

Standard Meaning: _____
_____

Initial Thoughts

Intuitive Interpretation

Emotional Response

How did this card play out today?

Evening Reflection

Date: _____   Deck: _____

Question: _____
_____

Card: _____

○ Upright   ○ Reversed

Keywords: _____
_____

Standard Meaning: _____
_____

Initial Thoughts

Intuitive Interpretation

Emotional Response

How did this card play out today?

Evening Reflection

Date: _____   Deck: _____

Question: _____

_____

Card: _____

    ○ Upright   ○ Reversed

Keywords: _____

_____

Standard Meaning: _____

_____

Initial Thoughts

Intuitive Interpretation

Emotional Response

How did this card play out today?

Evening Reflection

Date: _____   Deck: _____

Question: _____

_____

Card: _____

○ Upright   ○ Reversed

Keywords: _____

_____

Standard Meaning: _____

_____

Initial Thoughts

Intuitive Interpretation

Emotional Response

How did this card play out today?

Evening Reflection

Date: _____   Deck: _____

Question: _____

_____

Card: _____

◯ Upright   ◯ Reversed

Keywords: _____

_____

Standard Meaning: _____

_____

Initial Thoughts

Intuitive Interpretation

Emotional Response

How did this card play out today?

Date: _____   Deck: _____

Question: _____

_____

Card: _____

○ Upright   ○ Reversed

Keywords: _____

_____

Standard Meaning: _____

_____

Initial Thoughts

Intuitive Interpretation

Emotional Response

How did this card play out today?

Evening Reflection

Date: _____   Deck: _____

Question: _____

_____

Card: _____

◯ Upright   ◯ Reversed

Keywords: _____

_____

Standard Meaning: _____

_____

Initial Thoughts

Intuitive Interpretation

Emotional Response

How did this card play out today?

Date: _____   Deck: _____

Question: _____
_____

Card: _____

○ Upright   ○ Reversed

Keywords: _____
_____

Standard Meaning: _____
_____

Initial Thoughts

Intuitive Interpretation

Emotional Response

How did this card play out today?

Evening Reflection

Date: _____   Deck: _____

Question: _____

_____

Card: _____

◯ Upright   ◯ Reversed

Keywords: _____

_____

Standard Meaning: _____

_____

Initial Thoughts

Intuitive Interpretation

Emotional Response

How did this card play out today?

Evening Reflection

Date: _____   Deck: _____

Question: _____

_____

Card: _____

○ Upright   ○ Reversed

Keywords: _____

_____

Standard Meaning: _____

_____

Initial Thoughts

Intuitive Interpretation

Emotional Response

How did this card play out today?

Evening Reflection

Date: _____ Deck: _____

Question: _____

_____

Card: _____

○ Upright   ○ Reversed

Keywords: _____

_____

Standard Meaning: _____

_____

Initial Thoughts

Intuitive Interpretation

Emotional Response

How did this card play out today?

Evening Reflection

Date: _____   Deck: _____

Question: _____

_____

Card: _____

◯ Upright   ◯ Reversed

Keywords: _____

_____

Standard Meaning: _____

_____

Initial Thoughts

Intuitive Interpretation

Emotional Response

How did this card play out today?

Evening Reflection

Date: _____   Deck: _____

Question: _____
_____

Card: _____
     ○ Upright   ○ Reversed

Keywords: _____
_____

Standard Meaning: _____
_____

Initial Thoughts

Intuitive Interpretation

Emotional Response

How did this card play out today?

Date: _____   Deck: _____

Question: _____

_____

Card: _____

○ Upright   ○ Reversed

Keywords: _____

_____

Standard Meaning: _____

_____

Initial Thoughts

Intuitive Interpretation

Emotional Response

How did this card play out today?

Evening Reflection

Date: _____ Deck: _____

Question: _____

_____

Card: _____

◯ Upright   ◯ Reversed

Keywords: _____

_____

Standard Meaning: _____

_____

Initial Thoughts

Intuitive Interpretation

Emotional Response

How did this card play out today?

Evening Reflection

Date: _____   Deck: _____

Question: _____

_____

Card: _____

○ Upright   ○ Reversed

Keywords: _____

_____

Standard Meaning: _____

_____

Initial Thoughts

Intuitive Interpretation

Emotional Response

How did this card play out today?

Evening Reflection

Date: _____   Deck: _____

Question: _____

_____

Card: _____

◯ Upright   ◯ Reversed

Keywords: _____

_____

Standard Meaning: _____

_____

Initial Thoughts

Intuitive Interpretation

Emotional Response

How did this card play out today?

Evening Reflection

Date: _____   Deck: _____

Question: _____

_____

Card: _____

○ Upright   ○ Reversed

Keywords: _____

_____

Standard Meaning: _____

_____

Initial Thoughts

Intuitive Interpretation

Emotional Response

How did this card play out today?

Evening Reflection

Date: _____   Deck: _____

Question: _____

_____

Card: _____

○ Upright   ○ Reversed

Keywords: _____

_____

Standard Meaning: _____

_____

Initial Thoughts

Intuitive Interpretation

Emotional Response

How did this card play out today?

Evening Reflection

Date: _____   Deck: _____

Question: _____

_____

Card: _____

○ Upright   ○ Reversed

Keywords: _____

_____

Standard Meaning: _____

_____

Initial Thoughts

Intuitive Interpretation

Emotional Response

How did this card play out today?

Evening Reflection

Date: _____   Deck: _____

Question: _____

_____

Card: _____

○ Upright   ○ Reversed

Keywords: _____

_____

Standard Meaning: _____

_____

Initial Thoughts

Intuitive Interpretation

Emotional Response

How did this card play out today?

Date: _____ Deck: _____

Question: _____
_____

Card: _____

○ Upright   ○ Reversed

Keywords: _____
_____

Standard Meaning: _____
_____

Initial Thoughts

Intuitive Interpretation

Emotional Response

How did this card play out today?

Evening Reflection

Date: _____   Deck: _____

Question: _____

_____

Card: _____
   ◯ Upright   ◯ Reversed

Keywords: _____

_____

Standard Meaning: _____

_____

Initial Thoughts

Intuitive Interpretation

Emotional Response

How did this card play out today?

Evening Reflection

Date: _____   Deck: _____

Question: _____
_____

Card: _____

⭘ Upright   ⭘ Reversed

Keywords: _____
_____

Standard Meaning: _____
_____

Initial Thoughts

Intuitive Interpretation

Emotional Response

How did this card play out today?

Evening Reflection

Date: _____ Deck: _____

Question: _____

_____

Card: _____

○ Upright   ○ Reversed

Keywords: _____

_____

Standard Meaning: _____

_____

Initial Thoughts

Intuitive Interpretation

Emotional Response

How did this card play out today?

Evening Reflection

Date: _____ Deck: _____

Question: _____

_____

Card: _____

○ Upright   ○ Reversed

Keywords: _____

_____

Standard Meaning: _____

_____

Initial Thoughts

Intuitive Interpretation

Emotional Response

How did this card play out today?

Evening Reflection

Date: _____ Deck: _____

Question: _____

_____

Card: _____

○ Upright   ○ Reversed

Keywords: _____

_____

Standard Meaning: _____

_____

Initial Thoughts

Intuitive Interpretation

Emotional Response

How did this card play out today?

Evening Reflection

Date: _____   Deck: _____

Question: _____

_____

Card: _____

⊙ Upright   ⊙ Reversed

Keywords: _____

_____

Standard Meaning: _____

_____

Initial Thoughts

Intuitive Interpretation

Emotional Response

How did this card play out today?

Evening Reflection

Date: _____ Deck: _____

Question: _____

_____

Card: _____

◯ Upright   ◯ Reversed

Keywords: _____

_____

Standard Meaning: _____

_____

Initial Thoughts

Intuitive Interpretation

Emotional Response

How did this card play out today?

Evening Reflection

Date: _____   Deck: _____

Question: _____

_____

Card: _____

    ◯ Upright   ◯ Reversed

Keywords: _____

_____

Standard Meaning: _____

_____

Initial Thoughts

Intuitive Interpretation

Emotional Response

How did this card play out today?

Evening Reflection

Date: _____   Deck: _____

Question: _____

_____

Card: _____

○ Upright   ○ Reversed

Keywords: _____

_____

Standard Meaning: _____

_____

Initial Thoughts

Intuitive Interpretation

Emotional Response

How did this card play out today?

Evening Reflection

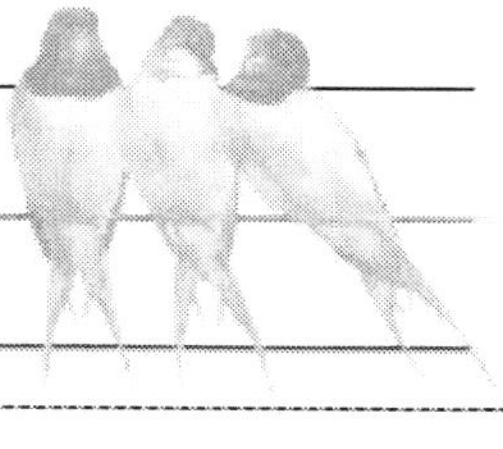

Date: _____   Deck: _____

Question: _____

_____

Card: _____

⭕ Upright   ⭕ Reversed

Keywords: _____

_____

Standard Meaning: _____

_____

Initial Thoughts

Intuitive Interpretation

Emotional Response

How did this card play out today?

Evening Reflection

Date: _____   Deck: _____

Question: _____

_____

Card: _____

○ Upright   ○ Reversed

Keywords: _____

_____

Standard Meaning: _____

_____

Initial Thoughts

Intuitive Interpretation

Emotional Response

How did this card play out today?

Date: _____   Deck: _____

Question: _____

_____

Card: _____
◯ Upright   ◯ Reversed

Keywords: _____
_____

Standard Meaning: _____
_____

Initial Thoughts

Intuitive Interpretation

Emotional Response

How did this card play out today?

Date: _____   Deck: _____

Question: _____
_____

Card: _____
○ Upright   ○ Reversed

Keywords: _____
_____

Standard Meaning: _____
_____

Initial Thoughts

Intuitive Interpretation

Emotional Response

How did this card play out today?

Evening Reflection

Date: _____   Deck: _____

Question: _____

_____

Card: _____

○ Upright   ○ Reversed

Keywords: _____

_____

Standard Meaning: _____

_____

Initial Thoughts

Intuitive Interpretation

Emotional Response

How did this card play out today?

Date: _____   Deck: _____

Question: _____

_____

Card: _____
○ Upright   ○ Reversed

Keywords: _____
_____

Standard Meaning: _____
_____

Initial Thoughts

Intuitive Interpretation

Emotional Response

How did this card play out today?

Evening Reflection

Date: _____   Deck: _____

Question: _____

_____

Card: _____

○ Upright   ○ Reversed

Keywords: _____

_____

Standard Meaning: _____

_____

Initial Thoughts

Intuitive Interpretation

Emotional Response

How did this card play out today?

Evening Reflection

Date: _____   Deck: _____

Question: _____

_____

Card: _____

○ Upright   ○ Reversed

Keywords: _____

_____

Standard Meaning: _____

_____

Initial Thoughts

Intuitive Interpretation

Emotional Response

How did this card play out today?

Evening Reflection

Date: _____   Deck: _____

Question: _____

_____

Card: _____

○ Upright   ○ Reversed

Keywords: _____

_____

Standard Meaning: _____

_____

Initial Thoughts

Intuitive Interpretation

Emotional Response

How did this card play out today?

Evening Reflection

Date: _____   Deck: _____

Question: _____

_____

Card: _____

    ○ Upright   ○ Reversed

Keywords: _____

_____

Standard Meaning: _____

_____

Initial Thoughts

Intuitive Interpretation

Emotional Response

How did this card play out today?

Evening Reflection

Date: _____ Deck: _____

Question: _____

_____

Card: _____

○ Upright   ○ Reversed

Keywords: _____

_____

Standard Meaning: _____

_____

Initial Thoughts

Intuitive Interpretation

Emotional Response

How did this card play out today?

Date: _____   Deck: _____

Question: _____
_____

Card: _____
   ◯ Upright   ◯ Reversed

Keywords: _____
_____

Standard Meaning: _____
_____

Initial Thoughts

Intuitive Interpretation

Emotional Response

How did this card play out today?

Date: _____   Deck: _____

Question: _____

_____

Card: _____

○ Upright   ○ Reversed

Keywords: _____

_____

Standard Meaning: _____

_____

Initial Thoughts

Intuitive Interpretation

Emotional Response

How did this card play out today?

Evening Reflection

Date: _____   Deck: _____

Question: _____

_____

Card: _____

    ○ Upright   ○ Reversed

Keywords: _____

_____

Standard Meaning: _____

_____

Initial Thoughts

Intuitive Interpretation

Emotional Response

How did this card play out today?

Evening Reflection

Date: _____   Deck: _____

Question: _____

_____

Card: _____

○ Upright   ○ Reversed

Keywords: _____

_____

Standard Meaning: _____

_____

Initial Thoughts

Intuitive Interpretation

Emotional Response

How did this card play out today?

Evening Reflection

Date: _____   Deck: _____

Question: _____

_____

Card: _____

⃝ Upright   ⃝ Reversed

Keywords: _____

_____

Standard Meaning: _____

_____

Initial Thoughts

Intuitive Interpretation

Emotional Response

How did this card play out today?

Evening Reflection

Date: _____   Deck: _____

Question: _____

_____

Card: _____

○ Upright   ○ Reversed

Keywords: _____

_____

Standard Meaning: _____

_____

Initial Thoughts

Intuitive Interpretation

Emotional Response

How did this card play out today?

Evening Reflection

Date: _____   Deck: _____

Question: _____

_____

Card: _____

○ Upright   ○ Reversed

Keywords: _____

_____

Standard Meaning: _____

_____

Initial Thoughts

Intuitive Interpretation

Emotional Response

How did this card play out today?

Evening Reflection

Date: _____   Deck: _____

Question: _____

_____

Card: _____

○ Upright   ○ Reversed

Keywords: _____

_____

Standard Meaning: _____

_____

Initial Thoughts

Intuitive Interpretation

Emotional Response

How did this card play out today?

Evening Reflection

Remember
to Stop
and Smell
The Roses

A lifetime fan of Diary & Journal creation for her own writing and embellishing, Helene Malmsio has compiled a collection of Diaries, Journals and Bullet dot grid Planners in paperback soft cover books for your pleasure. Check out Amazon "Strategic Publications" page for all the designs available in the series.

"When you use one of my Journals I want it to make you feel good. Knowing you can use these as a creative tool to craft a better life for yourself and your loved ones, is my inspiration – ENJOY!"

Other online resources from **Helene Malmsio** and **Strategic Publications**:

www.HeleneMalmsio.com
www.DiscoveryHub.net
www.PLRhub.net
www.ColourMeKind.com
www.Amazon.com/author/Strategic
www.lulu.com/spotlight/helenemalmsio

Thank you for your purchase of this book, as the bulk of the sales proceeds are used to help fund animal welfare organizations around the world, so you are helping to be the solution to a better kinder world when you buy from these resources.

And if you enjoyed this book, I would truly appreciate a simple comment in the book review section in the online sales page you ordered this book from.

"Be the change you wish to see in the world."
- Mahatma Gandhi

Strategic Services
Established in 1987

Made in the USA
Lexington, KY
11 December 2018